I0558990

"In Remembrance of Keeba Hardy, you are truly missed"

Niyonu's Victory
From Pain to Peace
Amidst The Global Pandemic

ASHANTI HARDY

www.LeesPress.net

Lee's PRESS

A Premiere Self-Publishing Services Company

This document is published by Lee's Press and Publishing Company located in the United States of America. It is protected by the United States Copyright

Act, all applicable state laws, and international copyright laws. The information in this document is accurate to the best of the ability of Ashanti Hardy at the time of writing. The content of this document is subject to change without notice.

ISBN-13: 979-8-9896434-4-8

Paperback

TABLE OF CONTENTS

ACKNOWLEDGMENTS

LORD, I thank you for your unconditional Love, your sufficient Grace, and endless Mercies. Without you, where would I be?

To my momma, Lorraine, where do I start? How blessed am I that God chose you to be my momma! Words cannot describe you, but if they could, I would be typing and talking all day, every day—just know that I love you, appreciate you, thank you, and am grateful for your encouragement and so many other things that I could go on and on about. I love you above and beyond!

To my daddy Robert in Heaven- thank you for your love, guidance, and lessons.

My siblings Andre' and Trice. God showed out when He made you two my siblings. So caring, compassionate, and loving. Thank you for being so amazing.

My siblings-in-love—Vi and Tim—you both have been such a blessing in my life. It feels as if I have known you two my whole life. Thank you both for being a brother and sister and loving me like my own siblings.

My nephews and niece—Jalen, Justin, Ryan, Joshua, and Lauren—you all don't know how much joy you've brought to my life. Thank you for your love.

To the best church in the land, my church family, Siloam Church International, and the best pastors in the land, Drs. Jonathon, and Sylvia Carter, thank you. Since 2005, Siloam

Church International has been my church home, and I have been truly blessed by Pastor and Co-Pastor Carter. To say that they are loving, compassionate, and kind is an understatement. Thank you, Pastor, and Co-Pastor Carter, for truly being a man and woman of God and being great leaders. Thank you to my entire Siloam Church family for being so encouraging and loving.

To Juan, your love, prayers, encouraging words, and motivation have been a blessing. I'm thankful for you being by my side.

To my friends who became family, you all are amazing. Thanks for being who you are.

DEDICATION

To my sweet sister Keeba—a brave, bold, and beautiful soul. To those who thought that the victory wasn't won, it was. To those who thought they didn't receive the victory, you did.

PREFACE

It was early 2020, the beginning of a pandemic that would spread worldwide. In all honesty, I wasn't even trying to write a book. Here in the United States, so much was going on, and to me, it was shocking how quickly everything happened.

I just started writing in my planner and then a notebook, and eventually, I began texting my sister Keeba daily, even though she was in the hospital with no access to her phone.

When I finally decided to write a book, I told Keeba that I would like for us to write it together so she could share what she'd gone through, and she agreed.

I felt like her story needed to be told to help someone else. I chose to use Niyonu, one of Keeba's middle names, in the title to showcase her uniqueness.

SISTER

A lover of GOD

A loving, smart, beautiful, organized, and dedicated daughter

A caring, amazing, and sweet sister

An awesome, kind, and admirable auntie

A devoted, thoughtful, and funny friend

A brilliant, engaging, and authentic author

An intelligent, passionate, and encouraging educator

A trustworthy, empathetic, and charismatic counselor

A knowledgeable, honest, and motivating mentor

SISTER was what I called her, BUT she was so much more to many:

A niece

A cousin

An all-around God-fearing woman who loved genuinely

THE JOURNEY BEGINS

3/23/2020 – 4/28/2020

Monday, March 23, 2020, was my sweet momma's birthday. Just five years prior, my mom and three siblings lost the wonderful man and leader of our family: my father and mom's husband.

Mom opened a few of her birthday cards and gifts that morning, but the pandemic was here, and things were different. It was just Mom, myself, and my sister Keeba. My brother (a physician) had recently bought an oximeter for us to check our oxygen levels regularly. Since Mom's levels were low, I called my brother, and he immediately told me to take her to the hospital. I then called my other sister and informed her that Keeba and I were taking Mom to the hospital. This was the beginning of the pandemic, so there were a lot of unknowns, but one thing that we did know was that everyone was pretty much staying in their own household if they could.

Keeba and I pulled up to the hospital and dropped Mom off at the ER entrance because, of course, no visitors were allowed during the pandemic. A big sign stated that only patients who were being seen were allowed inside.

We told Mom that we loved her before she entered the ER alone on her seventy-third birthday. My sister Keeba and I didn't want to leave the hospital because we thought our mom would be released later that day. Plus, I didn't want Keeba home by herself because she wasn't feeling her best. So, Keeba and I parked and updated our siblings that we had made it to the hospital.

We were both in the car, me in the front seat and Keeba in the back, with scarves over our mouths and noses, as per the health recommendations regarding the pandemic at the time. After all, it was just the beginning. We came prepared to wait, though; we had snacks and water and made sure we had our phone chargers.

The whole time we waited in the car, we texted and called our mom for updates, and she was in great spirits. She told us that she was fine and that she wanted us to go home, eat, and get some rest, but we refused to leave.

Meanwhile, my sister Keeba, in the backseat, coughed into her handkerchief often. At the time, I wasn't thinking that I should send her to the hospital as well. We were too focused on Mom at the moment.

I got out of the car several times just to get some fresh air. Around 8:00 p.m., after about seven hours of waiting, I received a call from Mom, stating that the hospital wanted to keep her because she had pneumonia. She apologized that we had been there so long. I said, "Momma, no need to apologize. Happy birthday again. We love you and just want you healed."

Keeba and I had a very long, quiet drive home. She and I were sad, tired, hungry, and surprised that they wanted to keep our mom in the hospital.

Soon afterward, our mom tested positive for COVID-19. During the time that our mom was in the hospital, Keeba and I were both working remotely, so that was a blessing in itself. We weren't too far from Mom's home or the hospital as we waited, hoping to receive a call that she'd be released soon.

It was difficult to focus on work, knowing that our mom was in the hospital alone. *At least she's in good spirits*, we thought. We talked to her every day, a few times a day, while she was there.

Over the next three days, several tests were run on our mom, and she was the same God-fearing, faith-filled mom that we had always known. She didn't change one bit. She still had jokes and still asked how we were doing, which was just the type of person she had always been and still is now.

In all my thirty-nine years, I had never seen my mom go to the hospital. I had also never known anyone so brave in my life. On March 26, 2020, I received a call from my mom that she was being released from the hospital. *PRAISE GOD!* I thought.

I went to pick her up in the same spot I'd previously dropped her off. She was prescribed pills to take for the next five days but had to quarantine for the next seven days.

On March 25, 2020, the day before I picked up Mom from the hospital, my sister Keeba went to get tested for COVID-19. They told her that her results would be back within three days and prescribed her some meds in the meantime.

I experienced déjà vu two days after picking Mom up from the hospital. My sister Keeba had shortness of breath, a persistent cough, and low oxygen levels. When I notified my physician brother about Keeba's levels, he told me to immediately take her to the ER, and I did—just as I had done for Mom only five days prior. Who knew that two days after picking my mom up from the hospital, I would take my sister Keeba to the same hospital?

Early Saturday morning on March 28, 2020, I told my sister that I loved her and let her out in front of the ER because visitors were still not allowed. I packed snacks and water in a plastic bag for my sister, but she was not allowed to take them inside the hospital. This time around, I did not wait in the parking lot. That, too, was another long and quiet drive home.

I went home to Mom's house because, even though my mom was doing better, she was still recovering, and I didn't want her to be home by herself for too long. While Mom was getting better, Sister (that is what I call my sister Keeba) was getting worse.

This was just the beginning of Keeba's journey.

For the first month that my sister was in the hospital, our family experienced roller-coaster-type emotions daily, ranging from sadness, happiness, fear, optimism, and so much more. Keeba, too, had been diagnosed with COVID-19.

She experienced so much in this month alone that it was unbelievable. She was put on a ventilator and had fevers off and on, plus low oxygen levels. Many procedures were done: a tracheostomy was placed in her throat, a bronchoscopy procedure removed mucus from her lungs, and, at one point, she was even in a medically induced coma.

Her tongue had swollen so big that she couldn't close her mouth. Can you imagine that? People still thought that this virus was a hoax, but this was just the beginning of the pandemic. This virus was and still is REAL!

THIS IS REAL

Some people said it was just like the flu. If they only knew all the pain that you went through. I think they would take it more seriously if they believed, *wow, this could really be me*. Some believed and still believe COVID-19 is a hoax, but please believe this is not a joke. I don't know what it must take for people to believe that this virus is not fake.

I am here to tell you the deal, it is a fact that this virus is real.

***

Early 2020 saw the beginning stages of COVID-19 spreading worldwide, and a lot was still unknown regarding this virus, much like it is today.

We were so grateful that we got to see Keeba through the Duo app and to see all the progress that she was making in the hospital, but it was still difficult to watch her go through the ups and downs that she experienced with this disease.

By April 19, 2020, she was still testing positive for COVID-19, and her fevers were still up and down. Cultures were done to see if she had a secondary infection, and she was given an antibiotic for it. Her blood pressure had gone down. Her white blood cell count was high.

By Monday, April 27, 2020, Keeba received her first NEGATIVE COVID-19 results. *PRAISE GOD!* We were overjoyed! Keeba had endured all the trauma her body faced with a smile.

THAT SMILE

Even after being in a hospital bed for one month, Keeba gave us a smile, and it wasn't a front. She couldn't even talk because her tongue was swollen, yet she still made us laugh. Keeba had us rollin'. Her strength was remarkable as she pushed through. This was just one of the many ways she would show everyone what she could do.

THE JOURNEY CONTINUES

4.29.2020 – 5.31.2020

During this period, my sister Keeba continued to fight. She needed the percutaneous endoscopy gastrostomy (PEG) procedure, where a tube is passed into a patient's stomach through the abdominal wall to allow nutritional fluids and medications to bypass the mouth and esophagus to reach the stomach directly.

Keeba continued to smile and to make progress despite all the blood being drawn and her confinement to a hospital bed. She patiently awaited admission to a rehab facility.

Meanwhile, as she got stronger, she received a little therapy at the hospital, which included occupational and physical therapy.

We were blessed to see her beautiful face through the Duo video app. We had so many laughs together, even throughout this ordeal. She wrote on a whiteboard to communicate with us, often saying she was hungry. She was so ready to have some solid food.

On May 7, 2020, around 5:00 p.m., my sister Keeba got the green light to be transferred to a rehab facility. *PRAISE GOD!* She was on the road to recovery after being in the hospital for over a month. Of course, for her to even be considered for and admitted to rehab, she had to have a negative COVID-19 test. We all were overjoyed because we thought this was one step closer to her coming home.

Before she left the hospital, she asked for a pen and paper to write an apology to one of the nurses because she had forgotten we had her belongings and thought the nurse had misplaced them. The very next day at the rehab facility, she wanted a Coke, so she wrote on her whiteboard, asking if she could have one. Then she got her first Coke in a long time. That was a really big deal because it was like a sense of normalcy for her.

REHAB

R = Recovered what you lost during a period of time.

E = Exercise is what you did at the drop of a dime.

H = Hardworking is what you were throughout your entire life.

A = Accomplished is what you became, even with all that strife.

B = Bravery is what you showed with everything you went through.

God said, *it is time for Me to show you something new*.

***

Sunday, May 10, 2020, was Mother's Day. It was another day that my sister Keeba was in the hospital, but another special Mother's Day for my mom to see her daughter through the Duo app. We told Keeba that it was Mother's Day because, being in the hospital for as long as she had been, Keeba had lost track of the days.

She told our mom Happy Mother's Day, but she had

a few questions. Keeba wanted to know when she would return to work. To give a little background information here, my sister Keeba was a school counselor at a middle school and was very dedicated to her career. She loved her coworkers and her students.

We told Keeba not to worry and that everything concerning her career was being taken care of but that our main concern was for her to get better physically. My sister Keeba was always about her business.

Another concern she had was whether she still had the virus. She had some memory loss regarding certain things, so she asked about that a few times. We informed her that she absolutely did not have the virus, that she was COVID-19-free, and that to even get admitted to rehab, she had to test negative for this horrible virus.

WONDERS

While Keeba sat in the hospital bed, she wondered what was ahead. Returning to work was on her mind. We all thought it would be just a matter of time.

Keeba wondered if she had the virus, and the answer was no. Keeba wondered, *why wasn't it time to go?* Keeba had so many things to wonder about while in that hospital bed.

So many thoughts were in her head, things that made her ponder, things that made her WONDER.

***

My sister Keeba had some rough days, where she

didn't sleep well. With all the different procedures that she had to endure and the facility's staff going in and out of her room at all hours of the night, it was hard for her to sleep. One procedure done was a T-piece procedure to supply her with supplemental oxygen.

The main thing Keeba wanted to do again was to sleep in her own bed.

Throughout her time at rehab, Keeba received speech, occupational, and physical therapy. She worked so hard but got frustrated while trying to make progress. Could you blame her? Of course, by this time, she had been in the hospital, then rehab, for about two months. Who wouldn't be frustrated and tired? We missed Keeba, and she missed us dearly. We were all ready for her to come home.

One day, my mom asked Keeba what she needed, and with a hand gesture, she replied *Money*. We all laughed at that sign. She was ready to be well and independent again. She asked the date and a few other questions about her being in the hospital.

When she found out that she had been in a medically induced coma, she was shocked and emotional. The first time we clearly heard her voice was on Sunday, May 17, 2020. Remember, her tongue was swollen at the beginning of this journey. So, until she got stronger, she had to communicate by writing on a whiteboard.

This day was very exciting because, even though her tongue was not completely healed, we understood what she said.

Throughout this ordeal, my sister Keeba stayed on top of her responsibilities. She asked about her bills, and we informed her that they were all taken care of. She was given another COVID-19 test a few days later, and again, it was negative. We were elated!

The speech and respiratory therapists came in and asked her questions like when her birthday was, what the current year was, and where she lived. She answered all their questions with ease.

The physical therapist came in to assist Keeba with sitting in a chair, which meant she had walked a little bit too. This was a big deal because she had been in a hospital bed since March 28, 2020. *PRAISE GOD!*

The therapist started Keeba on applesauce, but she couldn't move her tongue up and down to eat it, so they tried ice with her. Eventually, the swelling of Keeba's tongue went down because of the steroid medication she was given, which was another sign of the progress she was making.

On Sunday, May 24, 2020, Keeba's phone was brought to her. That was the first time she had had it since she'd been in the hospital. She made her first phone call since March 28, 2020, to one of her coworkers and friends, who Keeba had a friendly competition with.

Keeba was a Falcons fan; he was a Saints fan. I know you all can imagine how that discussion went. After she spoke with him, she read a lot of her text messages. Some of the posts from our brother's Facebook page were also read to her so she could hear all the prayers and love that family, friends, and many others had offered on her behalf. It was overwhelming.

Keeba was so grateful to see all that love shown to her. She said she could not wait to get out to tell her story.

My sister Keeba still had those restless nights and some rough mornings, but she did her best to keep fighting. She was making a whole lot of progress, too: sipping water, maintaining oxygen levels, exercising, and just improving day by day.

Considering where she'd started when she first arrived at the hospital, this was a MIRACLE. Things were definitely looking up, and we were happy about that.

Her speech sounded clearer every day. Toward the end of May, Keeba began sleeping a little bit better, and that made a big difference in her health.

Keeba asked about one of her favorite charities that she oversaw and collected donations for at the school where she worked. Despite all the suffering that my sister had endured, she always thought about others.

She asked Mom to find the donations that she had collected before she got sick and to send them off to the charity. That just showed the type of person Keeba was. Even though she forgot some things and had to be reminded of them, that was not one of them. God, through the Holy Spirit, brought that back to her remembrance.

Keeba started to brush her own teeth and complete

more therapy. The occupational and physical therapists helped her with standing and walking in place, using a walker for assistance.

During that time, Keeba was concerned about her job, and we informed her that she was fine, and that school was out because it was summertime. One day, she had a dream that she was going home, and she was so excited when she told us about it.

PEACE

Peace is the calm during the storm. It is actually what some people feel is not the norm. Having peace does not make you weak; it actually just shows you who you need to seek. Peace does not mean you have not experienced pain; peace is needed to remain sane.

THE VICTORY!

6.1.2020 - 6.23.2020

On Monday, June 1, 2020, my sister walked a little bit. That very next day, Tuesday, June 2, 2020, Keeba ate her first "real meal" in months. She had toast, eggs, grits, sausage, and orange juice for breakfast. Lunch consisted of a chicken potpie and more orange juice. Dinner was later that day, but she was just so happy to have food that did not come from a tube.

Also, during physical therapy that day, the therapist assisted her with walking. The very next day, my sister Keeba had some chicken, mac and cheese, greens, and a roll. She stated that, that was too much food. Keep in mind that she had been hooked up to a feeding tube for almost three months, so she had lost a lot of weight. Although she may have wanted all that real food, she had to get used to eating without the tube.

On Thursday, June 4, 2020, my sister's blood sugar rose, so she needed insulin. This day marked exactly four weeks of rehab for my sister. She took most of her meds by mouth that day, and she walked a little bit as well. I remember her saying that she had a taste for Church's fried chicken that day.

The next day, she sang a little bit, and that was music to our ears because we were used to her singing at any time, to any type of music.

I missed the Duo video call on June 6, 2020, but I

called directly to her room and talked to her, and I was so excited to do that.

We found out a little later that she was given another COVID-19 test over the weekend, and it, too, was negative. *To God be the glory!*

She had been having cramps, so she was given a CT scan (detailed images of inside her body), and we awaited the results. She had had some bleeding on her left side, and her hemoglobin (iron) was low. She had to get three units of blood from a blood transfusion. She was still fighting.

On Tuesday, June 9, 2020, Keeba was moved to another hospital and awaited transfer to another rehab facility. By this time, she felt better and was not cramping anymore. Her hemoglobin had also gone back up. She smiled a lot on that Duo call, and every time she smiled, we smiled with her because it was so infectious.

Even though she was in a hospital bed, she still had joy. Even though she was in a new hospital, the physical therapist and the occupational therapist came to her room and worked with her. This hospital had an actual rehab facility there, and we asked if Keeba could be approved to move to that floor.

Keeba watched a little TV at the last rehab place she was in but watched it a little more while she was in this new hospital. Of course, she saw lots of food commercials, and she wanted some of that food.

Although she was in a hospital bed, she still did the leg exercises that she had learned from her physical therapist.

If Keeba were approved for the rehab floor, the therapy would be more intense. The rehab that she was getting in her room at that time lasted only about twenty minutes with each therapist during her scheduled days for therapy.

We were waiting for the green light for her to be moved to the rehab floor. They had her doing breathing exercises, such as blowing in a tube, to strengthen her lungs.

She was approved to be moved to the rehab floor on Thursday, June 18, 2020. *PRAISE GOD!* Keeba knew that she would have to work a little harder, but it was worth it. On Friday, June 19, 2020 (Juneteenth—how fitting), she put on clothes instead of the usual hospital gown, and her chosen outfit was her Hardy Family Reunion 2018 T-shirt and sweatpants. She stood up in rehab. *Thank you, Lord!* We were so proud and excited.

On Saturday, June 20, 2020, my sister had physical therapy and occupational therapy. She was on her way, working hard in rehab. There was nothing that she could not do. We didn't get a chance to Duo with her that day, but I did call her because I had written a poem for her. It was untitled, and it still is. She cried and said that she loved it!

UNTITLED POEM
Hebrews 11:1, 13:5

Since you know that Faith is the substance of things
hoped for and the evidence of things not seen,

why won't you go ahead and let God take care of your
whole being?

He is right there in the midst of what you're going
through,

so just relax, be patient, and let Him do what He said He
would do.

He said that He would never leave you nor forsake you.
He will always be right there.

I know you already know this, but that is because He
cares.

I know you are tired, frustrated, and anxious, my dear,

but please remember that God has not given you the
spirit of fear.

He has given you the spirit of power, love, and a sound
mind.

But, if it is wisdom that you seek, surely you will find,

once you ask Him, of course, and He will surely provide.

Just a reminder that God is always on your side.

I know at times, you may think that He is not there,

but this is a reminder that He will always care.

****

Sunday, June 21, 2020, was Father's Day. Although our dad had passed away five years prior, it was still a special day! Keeba was so happy. She got to Duo with one of her best friends from high school, and that was a sight to see. You could see the joy in her eyes. It was very emotional.

On Monday, June 22, 2020, my sister stated that she slept well the night before. Her sleep patterns were still off, but she had some good nights' rest at times. As part of her therapy, Keeba sat in a wheelchair for about ninety minutes a day, but that day, she actually stood up for ten seconds. She was trying her best despite the tough times she experienced.

While I worked from home on Tuesday, June 23, 2020, my family and I received a group text from my brother stating that everyone should meet at Mom's house. My first thought was that he meant to send that to his wife, my sister-in-law, and accidentally sent it as a group text. I called my brother to see if it was a mistake, but I didn't receive an answer. Then, I received another group text.

Eventually, the whole family was at Mom's house, and my brother broke the news to us that our dear, sweet Keeba had gone on to be with the Lord that morning. We were shocked and devastated.

I remember seeing my mom and my eldest sister break down and cry. I was stunned as I sat on the sofa, quiet and dazed, trying to process what I had just heard. Then I broke down crying too. As I cried, I said to my family, "I told Keeba that we would write her story together once she got out of the hospital. She said OK, but now I must still tell her story." I'm not even sure what made me say that.

All the while, I was thinking, *A parent should never have to bury their child.* I instantly worried about Mom. Her heart must have broken into pieces. She had already lost the love of her life, my dad, in 2015, after forty-six years of marriage. Of course, I was heartbroken to lose my sister Keeba, but I am not a parent, so I could not fathom my mom's pain. I could only imagine that being a totally different type of hurt.

What was so shocking about our sweet Keeba passing away was that she was COVID-19-free, and she was in rehab, making progress. Of course, she was tired, and she even told us that she was tired. One time, she mentioned that she thought she would be a burden to us when she got out of the hospital. When she made that statement, we reassured her that she would not be a burden because we were family and we loved her.

We were so grateful that we got a chance to see Keeba through the Duo app and to see her smile through her pain almost every day as she went to different hospitals and rehab facilities. Keeba's extended family, colleagues, classmates, and friends were so kind and caring during her time in the hospitals and rehab facilities, even after she passed.

In the middle of a global pandemic, when so many

lives were lost, so much love was shown to Keeba, whether through a phone call or food, flowers, or cards being dropped off. People showed their love through so many thoughtful gestures.

I had always admired my mom's strength for as long as I could remember. Yet to see her during her time of grief while planning her child's funeral...was, to tell you the truth, I don't have the words.

Just know that my mom is a living angel. God called Keeba home; it was His will. She is now at home with Our Heavenly Father and our daddy. She was buried right next to him.

GOD IS LOVE

You are the light that shines so bright.

You are the love that is sent from above.

You are the peace that never seems to cease.

You are the strength that goes beyond any length.

You are God, and God is Love.

K-E-E-B-A

K = Kind is what you were to all those around you.

E = Educate is what you did, and we all learned from you too.

E = Encouragement is what you gave to people far and near, even to those who came around who needed to shed a tear.

B = Beautiful *bawse* (boss) is what you were, even at a young age—your book of poetry shows that; I could not wait to turn the page.

A = Amazing was your spirit; you cared for everyone. Your legacy lives on, and God said, *WELL DONE!*

HOME WITH THE LORD

Keeba, you told us that you were tired, and I guess we should've known.

It shouldn't have been a shock when God called you Home.

We miss you down here,

but we know you have no more fear.

No more pain in your body; it all went away.

We weren't ready for you to leave; we wanted you to stay.

We're grateful for the time we had with you,

but God decided it was time for something new.

***

My sister Keeba was not feeling well at all on Mom's birthday, but she still went to the hospital with me to drop her off. Keeba even made a birthday cake for Mom.

A few days before my mom went to the hospital, I decided that I would make her a cake for her birthday, so I went to the store to buy the ingredients. The day before her birthday, I decided that I would just buy a cake instead, so I went back to the store and bought a cake.

My sister Keeba decided that she would make the cake since I had already bought the ingredients (even though we had a store-bought cake too).

I know you may be wondering why I added this section toward the end and didn't have it at the beginning. Well, the reason that I am bringing this up is because, even though my sister Keeba was sick, she still made that cake for Mom's birthday. That was just the type of person she was.

Mom never got to eat any of those cakes because she was in the hospital, recovering from COVID-19, but the thoughtfulness of my sister Keeba mattered so much.

Around the end of March 2020, I also ended up getting COVID-19 while my mom recovered, and my sister Keeba went into the hospital. I had shortness of breath, no taste or smell, and felt weak overall. I was so grateful that I was able to work from home throughout the whole ordeal. My sweet momma took care of me after she recovered. What a blessing!

I wanted to let you all know that my sister won her battle with COVID-19. Even though Keeba had tested negative for COVID-19, the complications left behind by the virus would not let her survive. She was not defeated, though.

The Lord saw fit for her to go to His eternal house to be with Him. Keeba made such an amazing impact on people while she was physically here with us, and she has still been making an incredible impact.

Her legacy will live on forever. She was **VICTORIOUS** when she went from **PAIN to PEACE**!

ABOUT THE AUTHOR

Ashanti Hardy, originally hailing from East Point, Georgia, and currently residing in Riverdale, Georgia, is much more than just a daughter, sister, and auntie. With a diverse background in career advising and nutrition, Ashanti is a dedicated professional with a passion for making a positive impact in the lives of others.

A graduate of Fort Valley State University, Ashanti began her career journey in the field of Women, Infants, and Children (WIC) nutrition services, where she found fulfillment in empowering individuals and families to make healthier choices. Her commitment to serving in her community extends beyond her professional roles, as she actively participates in outreach initiatives at her church, Siloam Church International, and volunteers her time to support various causes.

Ashanti's latest endeavor holds a special place in her heart. Her forthcoming book offers a poignant glimpse into her sister's courageous journey through COVID-19, ensuring that her sister's legacy will endure and inspire others for generations to come. Through her writing, Ashanti continues to embody her unwavering dedication to helping others and leaving a lasting impact on the world around her.

www.ingramcontent.com/pod-product-compliance
Lightning Source LLC
Chambersburg PA
CBHW051251120626
46547CB00014B/1896